David Walsh

Premature burial

Fact or fiction?

David Walsh

Premature burial
Fact or fiction?

ISBN/EAN: 9783741197321

Manufactured in Europe, USA, Canada, Australia, Japa

Cover: Foto ©Andreas Hilbeck / pixelio.de

Manufactured and distributed by brebook publishing software
(www.brebook.com)

David Walsh

Premature burial

PREMATURE BURIAL:

FACT OR FICTION?

By DAVID WALSH, M.D.Edin.,

PHYSICIAN WESTERN SKIN HOSPITAL, LONDON.

"IPSIS REBUS COGNOSCERE."

LONDON:

BAILLIÈRE. TINDALL AND COX,
20-21 KING WILLIAM STREET, STRAND.

1897.

PREFACE.

"THE world," so some philosopher has said, "is mainly governed by prejudices." That saying will doubtless be true while so vast an untrodden field lies beyond the ken of man's knowledge. The task of science is to ascertain facts whereby reason may storm the strongholds of prejudice. Nothing is easier than to form conclusions from assumptions, which it is impossible, from what we as yet know of things, to verify. To think we know, to believe what we wish, and then to argue upon the thought and the assumption as facts—such are the inexact methods of sensational and emotional men. Surely it is time to carry to some court of reasonable scientific appeal the assertions of those who maintain the frequency of so terrible an occurrence as premature burial.

D. W.

Pump Court, Temple, London, E.C.
November, 1897.

PREMATURE BURIAL:
FACT OR FICTION?

OF all the terrors that could be flaunted in the face
of poor humanity, the fear of being buried alive
is surely the most ghastly. Unfortunately, as a
subject, it lends itself only too readily to showy and
telling treatment at the hands of alarmist popular
writers. It needs little literary skill to make its
grim tragedy seize upon the imagination with a grip
of iron. No wonder that the fear of such a fate, once
whispered in their ears, should fill the lives of nervous
folk with an ever-haunting dread. Yet, in spite of
the rank harvest of literature that has sprung up
around the subject, it may be at once stated that the
whole theory of premature burial is unsupported by
a single scientifically proved instance; that the
likelihood of such an occurrence is extremely small;
that the balance of probabilities weighs all in the
other direction; in short, that the whole of this
popular belief is nothing more than a legend. In the
following pages an attempt will be made to lay before
the reader in simple language the reasons that have
led to the foregoing sweeping conclusions. Many of
the arguments and so-called evidence in support of

the theory that premature burial is a common occurrence have been drawn from a recently published work by Messrs. Tebb and Vollum (a) which furnishes a complete and fairly concise statement of the matter from their point of view, Of late a great deal of prominence has been given to the subject in the newspaper press, and the subject has been more than once mentioned in Parliament.

So-called Counterfeits of Death.

A large slice of alarmist capital has been made out of certain conditions of suspended consciousness which are held to simulate death, and so to lead to hasty burial. The chief states thus dealt with are trance and catalepsy. which are really degrees of one and the same thing. In trance the vital functions are reduced to a minimum, and there is a more or less prolonged abnormal sleep, from which the sufferer, as a rule, cannot be aroused. In catalepsy there is the curious additional fact that the limbs, although motionless and passive, remain in whatever position they may be placed. In both conditions, however, there is the important fact that the vital functions, although they fall to a low ebb, are never altogether suspended. Thus, the breath comes and goes and the heart continues beating, facts that could not possibly escape a properly trained and careful observer; and, furthermore, although in these cases the skin surface may feel cold, yet the body temperature never falls much below the normal. The counterfeit of death by cataleptic conditions, then, is but a poor one, and not likely to pass as current coin among any but

(a) "Premature Burial." W. Tebb and E. P. Vollum, M.D. Swan, Sonnenschein and Co., London. 1896. P. 33.

grossly ignorant or careless observers. Here in England the body of a dead person is kept for four or five days to a week. Suppose a patient to be lying in a trance for that period of time, that is to say, cold and unconscious, but with respiration and circulation still going on. Can it be for a moment imagined that the attendants and friends, seeing none of the changes usual after death, would allow the body to be carried off to the grave? Yet we find in the book above alluded to the following passage :—" The existence of trance, catalepsy, and other death counterfeits, followed by hasty burial, has been alluded to by reputable writers from time immemorial; and while the veracity of these writers has remained unchallenged, and their narratives are confirmed by hundreds of cases of modern experience, the effect on the public mind has been of a transitory character, and nothing has been done either in England or America to safeguard the people from such dreadful mistakes." If that is the sort of assertion by which the writers of the work in question have to bolster up their case, then the apathy of the public of which they complain is hardly to be wondered at. The allusions of "reputable writers from time immemorial," however interesting, would not be taken as sound evidence in any modern scientific pursuit, as astronomy or chemistry, and a writer who gravely advanced such a contention would at once become an object of ridicule. It is quite true that scientific men have generally refrained from public discussion of the "narratives," which they seem to have looked upon as unworthy of serious attention. The evil, however, has become so great, and the efforts of the alarmists so widespread and persistent, that it is high time the scientific side of the questions were laid before the world. As to the above-quoted statement that the "narratives" have been "confirmed by hundreds of modern cases," the writer of the passage may be challenged to bring forward a single instance of premature burial that can be regarded as established by scientifically tested facts. Of loose evidence there is abundance—indeed, the book to which allusion has been made contains scores upon scores of such cases, but not one of them, as far as can be seen, bears the test of any really critical examination. In other words, as regards premature burial, an alleged occurrence that deeply affects the safety and comfort of the community, we are asked to surrender our judgment forthwith to a motley array of "narratives" coming for the most part from undertakers, grave-diggers, journalists, and other unskilled witnesses. Here and there we have a communication from a doctor, but the report is so general and so often based on hearsay evidence as to be practically worthless. Yet it is upon the strength of such untrustworthy statements that Messrs. Tebb and Vollum, who may be taken as types of the modern alarmist writers, advance the assertion that "scepticism, prejudice, and apathy on this subject have led to thousands of persons being consigned to the grave to return to consciousness in that hopeless and dreadful condition." (a)

FACTS OF THE CASE.

Let us now ask what are the essential facts of the case. Death, the common lot of all mankind, is often so gradual in its onset that one cannot always fix the precise moment at which it occurs. Its advent is marked by a number of sufficiently marked signs,

(a) Tebb and Vollum. *Op. cit.*, p. 180

that have been admirably discussed by the late Sir
Benjamin Ward Richardson in a paper entitled,
"The Absolute Signs and Proofs of Death." (a) Of
the tangible proofs of a real, as apart from an apparent, departure of life, the chief are—(1) Cessation of
respiration and circulation; (2) loss of lustre of eye;
(3) muscular relaxation and inability of the muscles
to respond to any stimulus; (4) fall of temperature;
(5) rigor mortis and putrefaction. Almost any one
of these signs, except putrefaction, if taken alone, is
open to fallacy. Thus, the act of respiration may be
so slight and faint as to become doubtful even to the
trained observer. The pulse may be so weak as not
to be perceptible to the touch, but it is unlikely that
any beating of the heart would escape detection by
an ordinary stethoscopic examination. More than
that, when a phonendoscope or other improved
modern instrument is used for auscultation it is
impossible to conceive that even the feeblest con-
tractions of the human heart could fail to be
heard. The muscles, again, respond to an electrical
stimulus now and then for so long a time as three to
ten hours after death. The cooling of the body may
be delayed from various causes, although the body is
nearly always quite cold in eight or ten hours at the
longest. But although it is freely admitted that any
one of these signs is apt to be misleading, if taken
alone, yet, on the other hand, when they are taken
together, not as isolated facts, but as phenomena of
common origin, then a mistaken conclusion could not
be made except as the result of gross incompetence
or carelessness.

Besides the signs mentioned in the last paragraph

(a) "Asclepiad," No. 21, Vol. VI., p. 6. 1889

there are others, of course, such as the loss of elasticity of the eyeball, which always comes on from 12 to 18 hours after death. If, at the end of 12 hours, any doubt exist in the mind of friends in the case of a body that has been laid out for dead, then it will be wise to call in consultation a second medical man, preferably, perhaps, one who can apply the electrical tests for muscle contraction. Certainly, such a step would be imperatively demanded if, after a day and a half, the eyeball had not softened and rigor mortis (cadaveric rigidity) had not set in.

The late Sir Benjamin Ward Richardson, like the logical man he was, went straight down to the root of the matter of premature burial by first making an exact study of the signs of death. His summary of the main points still holds good, and may be quoted for the comfort of the faint-hearted.

1. Respiratory failure, including absence of arterial pulsation, of cardiac motion, and of cardiac sounds.

2. Cardiac failure, including absence of arterial pulsation, of cardiac motion, and of cardiac sounds.

3. Absence of turgescence or filling of the veins on making pressure between them and the heart.

4. Reduction of the temperature of the body below the natural standard.

5. Rigor mortis and muscular collapse.

6. Coagulation of the blood.

7. Putrefactive decomposition.

8. Absence of red colour in semi-transparent parts. under the influence of a powerful stream of light.

9. Absence of muscular contraction under the stimulus of galvanism, of heat, and of puncture.

10. Absence of red blush of the skin after subcutaneous injection of ammonia (Monteverdi's test).

11. Absence of signs of rust or oxidation of a

bright steel blade, after plunging it deep into the
tissues. (The needle test of Cloquet and Laborde.)

"If all these signs point to death," is the practical
conclusion of this most philosophical writer, "if
there be no indications of respiratory function; if
there be no signs of movement of the pulse or heart,
and no sounds of the heart; if the veins of the hand
do not enlarge on the distal side of the fillet; if the
blood in the veins contains a coagulum ; if the
galvanic stimulus fails to produce muscular contraction; if the injection of ammonia causes a dirty,
brown blotch—the evidence may be considered con-
clusive that death is absolute. If these signs leave
any doubt, or even if they leave no doubt, one further
point of practice should be carried out. The body
should be kept in a room, the temperature of which
has been raised to a heat of 84 deg. Fahrenheit, with
moisture diffused through the air, and in this warm
and moist atmosphere it should remain until distinct
indications of putrefactive decomposition have set in."

Further Facts.

Next let us consider the usual course of things
after a death in a cool country like Great Britain.
The fact is certified by the medical attendant, or fail-
ing that, an inquiry is usually held by the coroner.
A weak point about the doctor's certificate is that it
can be granted without actual inspection of the dead
body. That flaw should certainly be remedied by
legislation, but before exacting further services from
the medical profession it would be well to arrange
for payment of an adequate fee. A member of any
other learned profession would flatly refuse to sign
an important document without remuneration for his

skilled services. By educating public opinion on these particular points those who live in fear of premature burial will be taking solid practical steps towards its prevention.

After death the body lies in the house for a variable number of days, usually about a week, and is not fastened down in the coffin, as a rule, until a short time before the funeral takes place. It is open all that time to the observation of many persons, such as nurses, undertakers, medical men, friends, and relatives, some of whom would be certain to note any departure from the usual signs of death. During this period, it need hardly be remarked, there would be ample space for breathing, a condition which would apply until the lid of the coffin was fastened down. Then we are faced with a simple physical problem. The ordinary coffin is air-tight, and any defect in that particular would be regarded as bad workmanship. The capacity for an adult varies, say, from eighteen to forty cubic feet, but the greater amount of that space is occupied by the body and its wrappings. Suppose a living person to be shut up in an air-tight chamber of the capacity mentioned, a few minutes, probably ten or fifteen at the outside, would exhaust all the available air, and suffocation would ensue. The tales, then, of unhappy individuals who have come back to consciousness hours after being shut up in a coffin may be dismissed as physically impossible. The only ways in which life could have been maintained under such circumstances would be:—(1.) The free admission of air into the coffin, a most unlikely thing considering the methods of manufacture usually adopted by undertakers. (2.) The assumption that life had been maintained for some hours without respiration, a supposition that cannot for one moment be seriously entertained, The only scientific fact, so far as one can see, at all approaching the latter hypothesis is the period of suspended animation after apparent death by drowning. In that state, life may sometimes be restored by artificial respiration when breathing has been stopped for several minutes. It is absolutely certain, however, that no such resuscitation would take place without the aid of vigorous stimulating measures to restore the suspended action of the heart and lungs. How an individual presumably weakened by illness and want of food is to have his breath suddenly restored to him in an air-tight coffin is a gordian knot that invites a vast deal of unravelling.

The cramped cubic space of an air-tight coffin disposes effectually of another common type of story where some unfortunate person is said to have been heard knocking or groaning for hours together after having been consigned to the grave.

One other point connected with the method in which funerals are carried out requires passing notice. There can hardly be a more unwieldy object to transport than a heavy coffin, not less on account of its shape and size than of its great weight. On the way from the bedroom to its resting-place in the cemetery it is exposed to all kinds of joltings and risks of upset. The trestles or table on which it stands may be knocked over by accident. The staircase may be narrow and winding, necessitating the use of slings, or even lowering from a window. Then there is the chance of a fall in lifting the coffin in and out of the hearse, or in letting it down into the grave. Lastly, the horses may fall down or run away. In this and other ways it is clearly possible that the body may become considerably shifted from its original position,.

and it seems reasonable to suppose that such may be more often the case than is generally suspected.

WHAT IS THE EVIDENCE IN SUPPORT OF PREMATURE BURIAL?

The assertion that persons are often buried while in a state of trance, so-called "death-counterfeit," has been already discussed. So far as that particular risk is concerned, it may reasonably be claimed that no such condition can be mistaken for death provided the ordinary tests be applied by a skilled observer.

The rest of the evidence may be gleaned from a consideration of the voluminous literature of the subject. It consists of an enormous mass of alleged cases gathered from the writers of all ages and from modern newspapers. A few typical instances of the former may be taken from Köppen's book, written in 1799, and entitled "Information relative to persons who have been Buried Alive." Under the heading of "England" he relates the following:—

"Lady Russell, wife of a colonel in the Army, was considered dead, and only through the tender affection of her husband was she saved from living burial. He would not allow her to be taken away until decomposition would absolutely force him to do so. After seven days, however, in the evening, when the bells were ringing, the faithful husband had the triumph to see her eyes open and her return to full consciousness."

There is a poetical ring about the foregoing story, but for all that, it could not be accepted as it stands as of any value beyond suggesting the desirability of further investigation of the subject. Viewed in the cold, dry light of scientific criticism, one would ask what condition any person would be in after remaining cramped up in one position for a week without food or water. Nor does the next tale, taken from the same source, carry with it any deeper sense of conviction :—

"*Leipsic.* — The wife of the publisher, Mathäus Hornisch, died, and, according to the custom of the times, the coffin was opened before being put into the ground. The grave-digger noticed golden rings on her fingers, and on the following night went to the grave to steal them—which he found was not easy to do— when suddenly she drew back her arm. The robber ran away frightened, leaving his lantern at the grave. The woman recovered, but could not make out where she was, and cried for help. No one heard her : so she got out of the grave, took the lantern, and went to her home. Knocking at the door, the servant called to know who it was. She replied, ' Your mistress. Open the door ; I am cold, and freezing to death.' The master was called ; and happily she was restored to her home again, where she lived for several years longer."

In this tale we find internal evidence, as the lawyers would say, of incredibility. According to the narrator, the poor woman had been shut up in a coffin and actually buried for several hours before resuscitation. As already shown by the physical laws of existence, so far as they are recognised by physiologists, life could not have been maintained under such conditions. Another defect in the story is that the supposed cause of death is not given. If we are to attribute the mistake to trance in the multitude of alleged instances where the morbid condition is not mentioned, then the cataleptic state must be infinitely more common than medical men generally suppose. In the next of Köppen's cases the cause of death is cautiously given :—

"*Stadamhof*, 1785. A young, healthy girl, on the way
to a wedding, had an apoplectic stroke, as it was thought,
and fell as if dead. The following day she was buried.
The grave-digger, who was occupied near her grave that
night, heard noises in it, and being superstitious, ran
home in a fright. The following morning he returned
to finish a grave he was digging, and heard the whining
again from the girl's grave. He called for help, the
grave was opened, when they found the girl turned over,
her face scratched and bloody, her fingers bitten, and her
mouth full of blood. She was dead, with evidence of most
dreadful sufferings."

This certainly does not tally with the usual course
of an apoplectic seizure, in which a patient lies unconscious, but breathing heavily, and on recovering
consciousness is more or less helpless and paralysed.
One would not expect a person so affected to regain
for a whole night the power of strong muscular movement, and of uttering loud noises when buried in a
coffin. Yet, this is the sort of evidence advanced by
Messrs. Tebb and Vollum in support of their views
upon premature burial, for Köppen's cases are quoted
in their book in a chapter headed "Duration of
Death Counterfeits." As they have not added a
word to show their doubt of the absolutely credibility
and value of Köppen's cases it must be assumed that
the latter are brought forward as constituting
in their opinion serious and authentic evidence.
A similar remark applies to the journalistic
stories which abound in the literature of premature
burial generally and in the book mentioned in
particular.

NEWSPAPER EVIDENCE.

The tales from this source are legion. They are of

a nature that offer an inviting field to journalists in search of sensational matter. Some types of " Our Foreign Correspondent's " contributions are the following : —

From the *Pall Mall Gazette*, May 11th, 1891.

"Narrow Escape from being Buried Alive.

A Penn Station telegram to Reuter says :— "A singular case of simulation of death from fright occurred here on Saturday. Mrs. Sarseville, the wife of a farmer in this county, was in the cow-house attending to the dairy work when she saw a nest of squirming snakes through a hole in the floor. She fell to the ground apparently lifeless from fright. Help was summoned, and she was carried into the house. Before the physician arrived Mrs. Sarseville had begun to turn black, he pronounced her dead, giving a certificate in which he assigned apoplexy as the cause. During the night, Mrs. Sarseville's daughter sat beside the coffin of her mother, lamenting her death. Just before daybreak she was startled to see the body move. She was more shocked when her mother opened her eyes and sat bolt upright in her coffin. The supposed corpse was no less startled than the girl to find herself dressed in grave clothes and lying in a coffin. Help was summoned, and the lady helped out of her narrow bed and into her ordinary clothes. She took breakfast with the family yesterday morning, and seemed none the worse for her ghastly experience."

This story, like many others of a similar complexion, comes from America. One cannot help being struck with the speed at which everything took place. Supposed death, certification, placing in coffin, night watch, resuscitation, and breakfast, all within twenty-four hours. Anyway, the tale, if ac-

B

cepted, would tend to show that a patient has a fair chance of issuing unaided from a death counterfeit. Another tale from across the Atlantic is gravely quoted by Messrs. Tebb and Vollum, the latter of whom, by the way, is an American. It is from the *Banner of Light*, Boston, July 28th, 1894, and runs :—

"COFFINED ALIVE!

" Sprakers, a village not far from Rondout, N.Y., was treated to a sensation Tuesday, July 10th, by the supposed resurrection from the dead of Miss Eleanor Markham, a young woman of respectability, who, to all appearance, had died on Sunday, July 8th.

" Miss Markham about a fortnight ago complained of heart trouble, and was treated by Dr. Howard. She grew weaker gradually, and on Sunday morning apparently breathed her last, to the great grief of her relatives, by whom she was much beloved. The doctor pronounced her dead, and furnished the usual burial certificate.

" Undertaker Jones took charge of the funeral arrangements. On account of the warm weather it was decided that the interment should take place Tuesday, and in the morning Miss Markham was put in the coffin.

"After the relatives had taken the last look on what they supposed was their beloved dead, the lid of the coffin was fastened on, and the undertaker and his assistant took it to the hearse waiting outside. As they approached the hearse a noise was heard, and the coffin was put down and opened in short order. Behold ! there was poor Eleanor Markham lying on her back, her face white and contracted, and her eyes distended.

" ' My God ! ' she cried, in broken accents. ' Where am I ? You are burying me alive.' ' Hush ! child,' said Dr. Howard, who happened to be present. 'You are all right. It is a mistake easily rectified.'

" The girl was then taken into the house and placed on
the bed, when she fainted. While the doctor was
administering stimulating restoratives the trappings o
woe were removed, and the hearse drove away with more
cheerful rapidity than a hearse was ever driven before.

      *   *   *   *   *   *

" ' I was conscious all the time you were making preparations to bury me,' she said. ' The horror of my
situation is altogether beyond description. I could hea
everything that was going on, even a whisper outside the
door, and although I exerted all my will power, and
made a supreme physical effort to cry out, I was power-
less. . . . . At first I fancied the bearers would not
hear me, but when I felt one end of the coffin falling
suddenly, I knew that I had been heard.'

" Miss Markham is on a fair way to recovery, and what
is strange is that the flutterings of the heart that
brought on her illness are gone."

There is a literary persuasiveness about the foregoing " narrative " that would carry conviction to
most folk, save the cold scientific critic. To the latter
it would seem strange that a patient in a state of
syncope from heart failure should be able to lie without nourishment for three days, and then recover only
some minutes after being fastened down in a coffin.
Again, what possessed the doctor, the undertaker,
and the friends, that they did not suspect anything
amiss from the absence of *post-mortem* changes in a
hot climate ?

Here is a tale from another part of the world, published in the *Undertakers' Journal*, August 22nd,
1893 :—

" SNATCHED FROM DEATH AT THE GRAVESIDE.

" A marvellous case of suspended animation is described from the British colony of Lagos, where an old woman named Oseni came to life when she was at the cemetery, about to be buried. The mourners had assembled at the cemetery, and, in accordance with the Mahomedan rule, the body was lifted from the coffin to be buried, when several distinct coughs were given by the supposed corpse. She was at once released from the clothes which bound her, and the old woman, to the surprise and amazement of those present, sat upright and opened her eyes. Some gruel was then procured, of which she partook with evident relish."

The following is a letter published in the *Daily Chronicle* of September 19th, 1896. It is to be found on page 101 of Messrs. Tebb and Vollum's book, and has more than a suggestive resemblance to another letter printed on the previous page, but which is signed "B. A.," and published in the *Lancet* of June 21st, 1884. The *Chronicle* letter runs:—

"Sir,—I infer from the following fact that numbers of persons are buried alive after being supposed to have succumbed to small-pox.

"Some years ago at St. Faul's, Belchamp, near Clare, a young man, who had been down with small-pox, was pronounced to be dead, and was put into a coffin, which fortunately was left unclosed until after the bell began to toll for his funeral, when he rose and stepped out. He lived for many years afterwards. In the same neighbourhood no less than three other similar cases occurred, saving that the undertakers were not so far forward with their work. Each of these would have been buried alive but for the facts that in one case the nurse, having suspicions, put a wine-glass over the mouth of the person (who had been already 'laid out'), and on returning in a quarter of an hour found it dimmed with breath; and that in the other case the mother of a mother, who with her baby was declared by the doctor to be dead, had blankets heaped on them, and after a while had the satisfaction of seeing them revive. Two of these three persons are, I believe, still living, and just past middle age. I enclose their names for your private perusal, that you may verify my statements if desired· The first-mentioned case happened about seventy years ago, but I heard of it from residents in the neighbourhood about forty years after it occurred.

" Nowadays, as soon as a small-pox patient is supposed to be dead, he or she is enclosed in a coffin and hurried off to the churchyard or cemetery the ensuing night—at least this is the practice in country places. I have no doubt that many have been buried alive.

" Yours faithfully,
" September 18th." " Ex-Curate.

With regard to this communication it may be observed that the reverend gentleman draws a very wide inference from slender premisses. What would the authorities of his college have said if in his early days he had attempted to justify a proposition of fact by hearsay evidence seventy years old ? Yet this kind of letter is considered good enough to insert at length in the pages of a book upon premature burial.

Some of the "narrow escapes" are quoted from medical journals; but, it may be remarked in passing, are not necessarily the more scientific on that account. As a rule, in these cases the editor simply inserts a paragraph reproducing, without comment, matter extracted from lay newspapers. It is clearly right for members of the medical profession to know the way in which a section of the outside world regards so interesting a topic as the possibility of live burial. In the *British Medical Journal* for March 12th, 1892, appeared the following :—

" A Narrow Escape from Premature Burial.

" The *Temps* publishes a case of premature burial prevented by the daughter of the supposed dead man, who, on kissing her father, perceived that his body was not cold. The funeral cortège was on the point of starting· Suitable measures restored the man to consciousness, and he opened his eyes and uttered two or three words. His condition is serious, but he is still alive. This incident occurred at Vagueray, near Lyons."

The *Lancet*, however, of Decembr 18th, 1858, contained the following account of a case of trance that came under the notice of a medical man, and seems credible enough :—

" The Dead Alive.

" (To the Editor of the *Lancet*.)

" Sir,—An article, 'The Dead Alive,' in your impression of the 27th ultimo, demands of me a veritable statement of the case alluded to. The subject of the inquiry is still living, and for some time past has afforded me scope for observation.

" I have only been waiting for a termination of the case, either in convalescence or death, to enable me to give to the profession, through your valuable columns, a full and truthful history of this rare and curious case, replete with interest. The exaggerated statement which has gone the round of the press has produced such great curiosity in this immediate neighbourhood that I have been applied to by many parties, professional and non-professional, to be permitted to see the case, the parents of the patient having refused admittance to all strangers.

" The case having extended over a long period, and fearing a detailed account might occupy too much of your valuable space, I have condensed the matter as much as possible ; but should the profession consider tho case worthy of a more enlarged history, I will gladly, at some future period, meet their wishes, as far as my rough notes, aided by my memory, will supply it.

"In August, 1858, I was requested to visit Miss Amelia Hicks, æt. 12 years and 9 months, daughter of a harness-maker, and residing with her parents in Bridge Street, Nuneaton. She was supposed to be suffering from pulmonary consumption. . . . . On October 18th, about half-past three a.m., she apparently died. She is said to have groaned heavily, waved her hands (which was a promised sign for her mother to know that the hour of her departure had come), turned her head a little to the right, dropped her jaw and *died*. In about half an hour after her supposed departure she was washed and attired in clean linen, the jaw was tied by a white handkerchief, penny pieces laid over her eyes, her hands semi-clenched, placed by her side, and her feet tied together by a piece of tape. She was then carried into another room, laid on a sofa, and covered over with a sheet. She appeared stiff and cold, two large books were placed on the feet, and I have no doubt she was considered to be a sweet corpse.

"About 9 a.m., the grandfather of the supposed dead went into the death-chamber to give a last kiss to his grandchild, when he fancied he saw a convulsive movement of the eyelid, he having raised one of the coins. He communicated this fact to the parents and mourning friends, but they ridiculed the old man's statement, and said the movement of the eyelids was owing to the nerves working after death. Their theory, however, did not satisfy the experienced man of 80 years, and he could not reconcile himself to her death. As soon as I reached home, after having been out in the country all night, I was requested to see the child, to satify the old man that she was really dead. About half-past ten, a.m., I was called, and immediately on my entrance into

the chamber I perceived a tremulous condition of the
eyelids, such as we frequently see in hysterical patients.
The penny pieces had been removed by the grandfather.
I placed a stethoscope over the region of the heart, and
found that organ performing its functions perfectly, and
with tolerable force. I then felt for a radial pulse,
which was easily detected, beating feebly, about seventy-
five per minute. The legs and arms were stiff and cold,
and the capillary circulation was so congested as at first
sight to resemble incipient decomposition. I carefully
watched the chest, which heaved quietly but almost
imperceptibly, and immediately unbandaged the maiden,
and informed her mourning parents that she was not dead.
Imagine their consternation! The passing-bell had
rung, the shutters were closed, the undertaker was on
his way to measure her for her coffin, and other necessary
preparations were being made for her interment. [The
writer then proceeds to give interesting details as to the
treatment of the case, and the means taken to promote
recovery.]

        "RICHARD BIRD MASON, M.R.C.S., L.S.A.
"Bridge Street, Nuneaton, December 14th, 1858."

The foregoing history points to the fact that a
living patient was laid out for dead for five or six
hours before anyone detected the error. It is plain
that the real state of affairs could not have eluded the
most cursory medical examination. That trance may
occur, and that now and then it may be mistaken
for actual death by careless observers is not
disputed. That such a condition is not easily
recognisable by skilled and careful inquiry, however, is a proposition that does not stand the
test of critical inquiry. It may be noticed that the
patient was apparently of that hysterical temperament commonly met with in phthisical persons. The

fact of a girl of twelve agreeing with her mother to wave her hands when about to die in itself furnishes strong internal evidence of a morbid mental state, and proves that the idea of death had a strong hold upon her imagination. The whole case simply shows how hard it would be for any one, even a weak, consumptive child, to be buried alive.

Another typical and seemingly authentic case of trance mistaken by unskilled friends for death is quoted by Messrs. Tebb and Vollum (a).

"In a lecture on 'Signs of Death and Disposal of the Dead,' delivered by Dr. A. Stephenson at Nottingham, January 8th, 1896, the lecturer said he once attended a girl living in that locality who was in a trance. All the preparations were made for the funeral, and the grave ordered. She remained in a trance three days, and her mother was annoyed because he would not sign her death certificate. On the third day she slowly rose and recovered. The girl would have been buried unless he had had a very great fear of her being buried alive."

The above is a further testimony to the safeguards that render burial while in a state of trance a practical impossibility. That proposition is supported by a case thus reported by Messrs. Tebb and Vollum (b). "No resuscitations are reported from any of these places, .e., the London mortuaries, except in the case of Ernest Wicks, who was found lying on the grass in Regent's Park apparently dead, and resuscitated in St. Marylebone mortuary (after being laid out on a slab as dead) in September, 1895, by the keeper, Mr. Ellis, assisted by Mrs. Ellis. When the doctor arrived the child was breathing freely, though still insensible. The child was taken to the Middlesex

(a) *Op. Cit.*, 97.
(b) *Op. Cit.*, 293.

Hospital, and was reported by the surgeon to be recovering from a fit."

In another part of their book the authors (a) mentioned say:—"The incident caused a good deal of comment, and suggested, doubtless, to the reflective reader that other cases of suspended animation might have a less fortunate issue." Quite so, but inasmuch as an unskilled person saw that the child was not dead, and that no other case of the kind (by the authors' own admission) has ever been known in a London mortuary, further reflection might suggest to the reader that such mistakes must be extremely rare, and their detection almost certain. At any rate, the responsibility of proving that anyone has been buried alive out of a mortuary rests with those who assert the frequency of live burial. Positive assertions of that kind demand positive proof.

A number of cases of sudden death are quoted by the advocates of the frequency of premature burial, because they imagine that such persons are liable to that particular misadventure. In this, as in all other forms of death, the fact may be ascertained beyond the shadow of a doubt by a properly conducted examination of the body. As to the suggested possibility of the suspension of life where all ordinary methods have failed to demonstrate its existence, no scientific medical man could for a moment seriously entertain such a theory. The inexact methods of alarmist reasoning are well illustrated by this assumption of a supernatural phenomenon in order to explain the original assumption of the constant occurrence of live burials.

The authors who have so often been quoted in these pages speak of the "imbecility of human judgment,"

(a) *Op. Cit.*, p. 315.

which they declare "exists now in an unmitigated
degree." Assuming, as may justly be done, that
their volume states the whole of the evidence in favour
of frequent premature burials, then one is somewhat
inclined to agree with them in their despairing view
of the general intellectual standard. At least, that
is the first feeling. After analysing the authors'
statements and illustrations, one finds them asserting
that, " the premature burials and escapes from
such disasters which are reported by distinguished
physicians and reputable writers, may be numbered
literally by hundreds, and for every one reported
it is obviously from the nature of the case that many
are never heard of." (a) Their estimate, however, is mild and moderate, compared with others
quoted by them. Thus Köppen records that a
" General Staff Officer, D.O. in D., states that, in his
opinion, one-third of mankind are buried alive." In
this case the persuasion appears to have assumed the
form of a monomania, and Messrs. Tebb and Vollum
are constrained to add that, "This estimate is
obviously exaggerated, although many trustworthy
experiences prove that a certain number of those who
die have returned to consciousness in their graves."
Mr. John Smart, in his "Thesaurus," pp. 26-28,
London, 1817, has wisely adopted a non-committal
attitude. " The number of dreadful catastrophes," he
writes, "arising from premature interment. . . . that
have been *discovered* only, or have transpired to many
above ground, both in ancient and modern times,
conveys to every reflecting mind the fearful thought
that they are but a *sample* (per synecdochen) out of
such an incalculable host, perhaps one in a thousand."
The Rev. J. G. Ouseley, in a pamphlet on " Earth to

(a) *Op. Cit.* p. 19.

Earth Burial," London, 1895, estimates "that two thousand seven hundred persons, at least, in England and Wales are yearly consigned to a living death, the most horrible conceivable." The Rev. Walter White, in the "Disorder of Death," 1819, p. 362, quotes from a report, "Monsieur Thieurey, Doctor Regent of the Faculty of Paris, is of opinion that one-third, or perhaps half, of those who die in their beds are not actually dead when they are buried. He does not mean to say that so great a number would be restored to life. In the intermediate state, which reaches from the instant of apparent death to that of total extinction of life, the body is not insensible to the treatment it receives, though unable to give any signs of sensibility." This passage is printed as it stands in Messrs. Tebb and Vollum's book (p. 222). It may be suspected that, like many distinguished Frenchmen, M. Thieurey was of Irish descent, which would account for the strange statement that a proportion of those who die in their beds are not actually dead when they are buried." Dr. Léonce Lénormand has given his deliberate opinion "that a thousandth part of the human race have been, and are, for want of knowledge, annually buried alive." This Messsrs. Tebb and Vollum regard "as an under, rather than over, estimate." Lastly, Mr. Le Guenu reckons the number of premature burials in France at two per thousand. In view of these conclusions one is led to agree with the above-mentioned reflection as to the imbecility of human judgment with which the writers credit their readers, and to crave for more light, so that one may discover whither the imbecility leads, for that way lies mitigation.

The Theory of Frequent Premature Burial Unsupported by any Eminent Scientific Men.

One strong point against the occurrence of frequent
live burial is that such a proposition has had the support of no really first-rate scientific men, medical or
otherwise. It is true that such names as those of
Professor Ferrier, Sir Henry Thompson, and the late
Sir Benjamin Ward Richardson are scattered freely
through the literature of the subject, but inquiry
shows that their authority is always quoted on some
side issue, such as the signs of death or the value of
cremation. The probability of premature burial has
been before the world for many centuries, and by this
time, if there had been any truth in the matter, it
would certainly have received the sanction of some
strong man of science. As it is, we look in vain for
the endorsement of any such eminent leader whose
name would be a guarantee that he had carefully
sifted facts and weighed arguments before arriving
at his conclusions.

This trick—for it is nothing else—of bringing
the names of well-known men into an argument re-
gardless of the purport of their actual words, has
recently been carried to an amusing extreme in the
public press of this country. The advocates of the
premature burial theory have published in every
newspaper that has afforded them the hospitality of
its columns letters containing passages more or less
exactly resembling the following, which is taken from
the *Daily Chronicle*. After stating that the subject has
arrested the attention of men of light and leading,
both at home and abroad, the writer proceeds:—"Mr.
Gladstone writes: ' I am very sensible of the interest
attaching to the subject'; Mr. Bayard, late United

States Ambassador, writes that 'the subject is certainly of great interest and importance'; the Bishop of London says, ' The subject is one to which you are justified in calling attention '; Count Kornice Karnicki (Chamberlain to the Tsar), who has been instrumental in rescuing [a young lady from premature interment, writes: 'I am astonished that anyone should be insensible of its paramount importance.' " These expressions are, with the exception of the last, non-committal, polite, and meaningless. The last-mentioned can hardly be said to come from a well-known man, and one does not, as a rule, look for weighty scientific testimony from a Russian courtier; when examined, however, it proves to be nothing more than a vague and indirect expression of personal opinion. A strong cause would hardly require bolstering up by pressing unwilling recruits into its service in this fashion.

POSSIBILITY OF PREMATURE BURIAL.

The possibility of live burial, apart from its probability, must be limited. Not a frequent possibility, but a remote contingency, that can occur only, as insisted upon again and again in these pages, under circumstances of culpable carelessness. With a systematic medical examination of the body before death it cannot be admitted that the premature burial of a live person will ever take place. The collapsed contions that simulate death may be due to trance, to cholera, and to other exhausting diseases, especially in patients of neurotic temperament. Cataleptic seizures are comparatively rare, and when they do occur, do not cause cessation of respiration and circulation, and so cannot elude skilled examination.

The greatest real danger appears to lie in hasty burial, which may be necessitated in hot countries by the rapid onset of putrefactive changes. In such cases the friends may adopt the obvious precaution of not allowing the body to be removed until the process in question has commenced. Dead bodies are often quickly buried during epidemics of infectious disease, and there can be little doubt that in time of plague, cholera, and the like, bodies are occasionally removed while still alive. Nor can it be denied that a similar risk confronts those wounded in battle, whether by sea or land.

How to Obtain Scientific Evidence of Premature Burial.

At this point it may be asked what sort of evidence would satisfy the demands of a scientific investigator before he accepted the proposition of frequent premature burial. Clearly he would want proof, absolutely logical and convincing proof, that in a large number of instances people had been found alive in their graves or under circumstances that left no doubt as to their having been alive in that dreadful position. The chief presumptive proofs advanced by the alarmists, gathered from their numerous narratives, are the sounds issuing from the grave, change of position of the body, and signs of violent struggle. Now, in the nature of things it has been shown that no one could live more than a few minutes inside an air-tight coffin, and much less so when covered with several feet of earth, so that no faith can be placed in the accounts of sounds issuing from a coffin more than, say, ten or fifteen minutes after it has been fastened down. The alteration of the position of a body

inside a coffin may be explained in the various ways
adoped in the carriage of so cumbersome an object.
The contorted expression of face is common in some
modes of death and a body is sometimes buried
stiffened out in the attitude assumed in the last
struggles. These and other fallacies will have to be
carefully guarded against, and the previous history
and last illness of the sufferer taken into account.
If a fairly credible case be made out it will have to
be borne out by many others equally well attested.

The Books Upon Premature Burial.

Unsatisfying " narratives " of the kind above discussed abound in the books written upon this
subject, and they are apparently inserted as proofs
of the theory they advance. Their precise value for
that purpose may be now to some extent gauged by the
reader of these pages. However, lest there be any
lingering doubt in his mind that the matter has been
dealt with in a perfectly candid spirit, he is invited to
pay careful attention to the following amusing instance
of anxiety to pile up evidence at any cost. In the book
so often quoted, reference is make to cases of fakirs
buried alive for a month or more, deprived of light,
air and food, and dug out uninjured at the end
of that time. The names of several gentlemen are
mentioned as willing, from personal observation, to
assert that the occurrences took place without col-
lusion or deception. At this point Messrs. Tebb and
Vollum take up the parable, as follows.

" A case of this kind was exhibted at the Westminster
Aquarium in the autumn of 1895, which was carefully
witnessed and tested by medical experts, without detection of any appearance of fraud or simulation. The

hypnotised man, Walter Johnson, an ex-soldier, twenty-nine years of age, was in a trance which lasted thirty days, during which time he was absolutely unconscious, as shown by the various experiments to which he was subjected.

" A case of induced trance and experimental burial, not unlike that of the Indian fakirs referred to, was reported in the London *Daily Chronicle*, March 14th, 1896. The experiment was carried out under test conditions."

" Buried Alive at the Royal Aquarium.

" After being entombed for six days in a hypnotic trance, Alfred Wootton was dug up and awakened at the Royal Aquarium (Westminster), on Saturday night in the presence of a crowd of interested spectators. Wootton was hypnotised on Monday by Professor Fricker, and consigned to his voluntary grave, nine feet deep, in view of the audience, who sealed the stout casket or coffin in which the subject was immured. Seven or eight feet of earth were then shovelled upon the body, a shaft being left open for the necessary respiration, and in order that the public might be able to see the man's face during the week. The experiment was a novel one in this country, and was intended to illustrate the extraordinary effect produced by the Indian fakirs, and to demonstrate the connection between hypnotism and psychology, while also showing the value of the former art as a curative agent. Wootton is a man æt. thirty-eight, he is a lead-worker, and on Monday weighed 10 st. 2½ lbs. He had previously been in a trance for a week at Glasgow, under Professor Fricker's experienced hands, so was not altogether new to the business ; but he is the first to be 'buried alive' by way of amusement. To the uninitiated the whole thing was gruesome in the

(a) *Cp. Cit.*, p. 48.

extreme, and this particular form of entertainment certainly cannot be commended. Before being covered in Wootton's nose and ears were stopped with wax, which was removed before he was revived on Saturday. The theory of the burial is to secure an equable temperature day and night—which is impossible when the subject is above ground in an ordinary way—and therefore to induce a deeper trance. Of, course, too, the patient was out of reach of the operator, and no suspicion of continuous hypnotising could rest upon the professor. No nourishment could be supplied for the same reason, though the man's lips were occasionally moistened by means of a damp sponge on the end of a rod, and no record of temperature or respiration could be kept. A good many people witnessed the digging up process, and the awakening took place in the concert room, whither the casket and its burden were conveyed. The professor was not long in arousing his subject after electric and other tests had been applied to convince the audience that the man was perfectly insensible to pain and everything else. Indeed, a large needle was run through the flesh on the back of the hand without any effect whatever. The first thing on regaining consciousness that Wootton said was that he could not see, and then he asked for drink—milk, and subsequently a little brandy, being supplied. As soon as possible the patient was lifted out of his box, and with help was quickly about the platform. He complained of considerable stiffness of the limbs, and was undoubtedly weak, but otherwise seemed none the worse for his remarkable retirement from active life, and abstention from food for nearly a week. He was swathed in flannel, and soon found the heat of the room very oppressive, though at first he appeared to be particularly anxious to have his overcoat and his boots. It is anticipated that, in a day or two at most, Wootton will have regained his usual vigorous health."

This case, which Messrs. Tebb and Vollum thought sufficiently well attested to take an early and prominent place in their book. Its sequel may be gathered from the following report, copied from *Reynolds's Newspaper* of May 16th, 1897:—

"HYPNOTISM EXTRAORDINARY.

"TOURING IN A COFFIN.

"An extraordinary action engaged the attention of Judge Emden at Lambeth County Court on Wednesday. Frederick Charles Howard, a young man, residing at 35 Bellenden Road, Peckham, sued 'Professor' Fricker, who is well known in connection with hypnotism and trances, for £8 7s. for unpaid wages.

"Mr. A. H. Williams, solicitor, appeared for the plaintiff, who, in his evidence, stated that he got into correspondence with the 'professor' through replying to an advertisement. In September he became engaged to the 'professor' as a subject for his hypnotic experiments, and on the understanding that he would act in a trance. His salary was fixed at £2 per week.

"Plaintiff went at considerable length into his experiences. Luton was the first town he visited, and the show had been well advertised there. He (plaintiff) was placed in a coffin at Euston Station, presumably in a trance, and was then conveyed to Luton Station, from whence he was removed, coffin and all, to the Town Hall. This was performed to the accompaniment of the music of a brass band. (Laughter.) That took place on a Monday. At seven o'clock the same evening he awoke, and was later in the evening put to sleep for the remainder of the week. The public were told that he had been sleeping forty days and forty nights, and that he was going round England like this.

"Judge Emden: What! in the coffin?

"Plaintiff: Yes; in the coffin. Unfortunately, business was bad, and it was ultimately arranged between the 'professor' and the manager that the former should disappear, and the announcement be made that he (plaintiff) was dead.

"Judge Emden: You were still in the coffin?

"Plaintiff: Yes, your honour. This idea was carried out. (Laughter.) There and then the police and the doctor were sent for, the 'professor' in the meantime keeping himself within doors. (Laughter.) It was about ten o'clock in the morning when the doctor came accompanied by the police inspector. He felt the doctor feel his pulse and lift him up—(laughter) and he heard the police inspector say to the doctor, ' What shall we do with him? Shall we order him to the hospital or the mortuary?' (Laughter.) The doctor replied that it was ' No good taking him to the hospital, for if he was in a trance they could do nothing for him there.' (Laughter.) To that the police inspector remarked, ' If he is dead, we shall have to get the " professor's " body. Just as he was about to be taken to the mortuary the 'professor' arrived, and said he would put everything right. He said that he (plaintiff) only had the toothache. (Loud laughter.) It was then arranged that he should then lay on until the following Saturday, when the 'professor' should tap him three times on the head and he would awake. This plan was also carried out, and when Saturday arrived the show was well patronised by the public. At the moment of his waking, the brass band, according to previous arrangement, played up " See the conquering hero comes." (Roars of laughter, in which plaintiff joined.)

"Judge Emden said the allegations were of a serious character. He, however, was not there to decide whether or not defendant, as was alleged, was practising a gross imposition upon the public. Plaintiff had made out his case for salary, and there must be judgment for the amount claimed.

"The 'Professor' declined to answer certain questions put to him by Mr. Williams, and, addressing his honour, exclaimed, 'I shall appeal against this judgment!'

"Judge Emden: It may be useful to you to know that there is an order for immediate payment, and that you cannot appeal without my leave.

"The 'Professor' left the court."

Messrs. Tebb and Vollum cannot be congratulated on the upshot of their report of "Professor" Fricker's performances. Nor can a better fate be anticipated for those who seek for evidence upon scientific matters from jugglers in public places of amusement. As a scathing commentary upon the value of a scissors and paste collection of loose evidence, the above incident is unique. After this, it seems hardly needful to quote or discuss any more of the unending array of ghastly narratives which sway the emotions rather than convince the reason, and which fail to bring forward evidence that would be accepted in an ordinary scientific investigation. The alarmists spring upon the world a startling conclusion as the extreme frequency of premature burial, and the least they can do is to produce sound and positive evidence of their assertions.

As an illustration of the fallacies that surround the signs of death we may take the single one of the fall of temperature. In noting that sign the scientific observer will bear in mind the following facts:—(a)

"The temperature of the body at the time of death is retained for some time. Cooling will depend on the medium in which the body is placed, and mere coldness of the body is not a sign of death. Average

(a) "Forensic Medicine." H. A. Husband, M.D. Edinburgh, 1895. 6th Edition, p. 32

temperature of the body during life 98° to 100° F."

1. Fat persons retain the heat longer than thin ones; adults longer than children or old persons. Bodies are cooled by—1, Radiation; 2, Conduction; 3, Convection.

2. Bodies immersed in water cool more rapidly than in air. This fact may be of importance in determining survivorship in a case of drowning.

3. Bodies in bed and under the clothes, or covered in other ways, cool less rapidly than when exposed.

4. Persons killed by lightning keep longer warm than others. (?)

5. Death by suffocation retards the process of cooling.

6. The body may be cold externally, but possesses a considerable amount of heat when the internal organs are exposed. Persons who have died of cholera, yellow fever, or suddenly of some acute disease—rheumatism— may retain for some hours a considerable amount of heat. It has even been asserted that in some diseases—cholera —there is an increase of temperature soon after death.— (Laycock).

7. Most bodies, under ordinary circumstances, are, as a rule, quite cold in from eight to twelve hours after death.

A scientific report of a supposed case of premature burial might be based upon some such form as the following:—

Name, age, sex, and occupation of person alleged to be dead. Appearance of body at time (a) of supposed death, (b) of burial, (c) of exhumation.

Previous history, family and personal, circumstances attending supposed death (sickness, accident, duration, medicines, nursing, convulsions, &c.), name and address of medical attendant, and length of attendance. Full description by doctor of illness and

mode of supposed death. Copy of death certificate.
Report of nurse and friends present at time of supposed death. Full description from all sources of the
condition of the body between the time of the supposed death and the closing down of the coffin.
Medical report of the same, including a systematic
description of the various signs of death, the methods
adopted to test each of them, and the order of their
appearance. All medical evidence to be corroborated,
if possible, by that of a second medical man. The
surroundings of the body as to temperature, clothing,
moisture, &c., to be noted. The kind of coffin to be
described, its position, material, size, and whether air-
tight or not. The exact moment of fastening down
lid of coffin to be noted, together with the time and
method of removal. Full particulars of grave, and
time of burial. Full statement of evidence on which
assertion of live burial was based. Names and
addresses of all persons who can testify to these
points, and note of all corroborative facts bearing
upon the same directly or indirectly. Full names and
addresses of all concerned in any way.

By the adoption of some such plan as the foregoing, it would be possible to hope for fairly credible
evidence one way or the other. But, as already
hinted, the establishment of a single case of premature burial would hardly be sufficient. Quite possibly
the evidence of some of the principal witnesses might
be misleading, not of intent, but because they had
not been trained to careful and exact observation. A
number of cases would have to be proved to carry
conviction. When writers come forward with alarm-
ing positive assertions as to the frequency of premature burial, one naturally expects them to produce
convincing proof of the soundness of the position.

So far from that being the case, however, we fail to
find in all the instances adduced a single one that
from the point of view of absolutely sound evidence
has, to use a homely phrase, the value of a brass
farthing.

SUGGESTED METHODS OF PREVENTION.

If once the probability of premature burial were
proved there could be no general hesitation in
adopting stringent measures to prevent such a
calamity. As it is the logical chain is incomplete;
the alarmists wish us to move Parliament to legislate
to prevent a terrible social danger, but they have not
gone through the necessary preliminary of proving
that the danger exists. Many unthinking persons,
moved by the ghastly terrors of the assumed tragedy,
have racked their brains to find ways of helping
resuscitated victims to leave the coffins to which they
have been consigned.

A most ingenious plan, but at the same time quite
fallacious, suggested by Mr. de Parville, appeared in
an article in *All the Year Round*, July, 1869. *(a)*

" Mr. de Parville now announces the possibility of this
great desideratum (a rapid and accurate test of death).
He professes to place in any one's hands a self-acting
apparatus, which would declare not only whether the
death be real, *but would leave in the hands of the* experimenter a written proof of the reality of the death. The
scheme is this: It is well-known that atropine—the

tive principle of belladonna—possesses the property of
considerably dilating the pupil of the eye. Oculists
constantly make use of it when they want to perform
an operation, or to examine the interior of the eye. Now

(a) Quoted by Messrs Tebb and Vollum, p. 273.

M. le Docteur Bouchut has shown that atropine has no action on the pupil when death is real. In a state of lethargy the pupil, under the influence of a few drops of atropine, dilates in the course of a few minutes; the dilatation also takes place a few instants after death; but it ceases absolutely in a quarter of an hour, or half an hour at the very longest; consequently, the enlargement of the pupil is a certain sight that death is only apparent.

"This premised, imagine a little camera obscura, scarcely so big as an opera glass, containing a slip of photographic paper, which is kept unrolling for five-and-twenty or thirty minutes by means of clockwork. This apparatus, placed a short distance in front of the dead person's eye, will depict on the paper the pupil of the eye, which will have been previously moistened with a few drops of atropine. It is evident that, as the paper slides before the eye of the corpse, if the pupil dilate, its photographic image will be dilated; if, on the contrary. it remains unchanged, the image will retain its original size. An inspection of the paper then enables the experimenter to read upon it whether the death is real or apparent only. This sort of declaration can be handed to the civil officer, who will give a permit to bury in return."

The test is good enough so far as it goes. Atropine will dilate the pupil of the living eye, provided it be not immovable as the result of disease. But atropine will do more than that, for it will cause the contraction of a pupil for some time after death, up to ten or according to some authorities, even twenty hours. Mr. de Parville himself admits that expansion may be produced up to half an hour after death. His test, then, would be useless until twenty hours after apparent death. The fact is that the iris is essentially composed of muscular structure, and obeys the general law of that particular tissue in responding to local stimuli up to ten or twenty hours after the cessation of life.

A scientific test for death, recently suggested by
M. Icard, (a) depends on the proportion that the
only certain proof is the absolute cessation of circulation. The absolute proof of the maintenance of the
latter, he takes to be absorption. He found experi-
mentally that ten grains of fluorescin are more than
enough to produce a characteristic colouring reaction
in the living adult. He, therefore, proposed to
inject under the skin of the person to be tested two
drachms of a ten per cent. solution, which, if
circulation were present, would speedily give rise to
an emerald green discolouration of the cornea and
the skin. This appears to be one of the most
scientific tests hitherto introduced.

From time to time numerous devices have been
brought forward with a view of enabling prematurely
buried persons to escape from their painful position.
Of late, one of these has been widely advertised in
this and other countries. It was invented by Count
Karnice-Karnicki, a gentleman already alluded to in
these pages, and has been described as (b) follows :—

" After many attempts, he has succeeded in
inventing an apparatus consisting of a hermetically-
closed iron box, which is placed on the top of the
grave, and is connected with the coffin by a hollow,
easily-removable tube. Inside this tube is a spring,
which at one end is connected with the iron box,
and to the other end, inside the coffin, is affixed a
glass ball, so that it just touches the chest. The
faintest movement of this ball, as a [result of the
slightest movement of the body, or even of the
simple motion of breathing, suffices to cause the

(a) Reviewed in *La Médecine Moderne*,—February 24th, 1897.
(b) Premature Burial and its Prevention. A Circular of the
Society for the Prevention of Premature Burial.—1897.

lid of the iron box to spring open and a flag to rise
perpendicularly about four feet above ground.
At the same time a strong alarum bell is rung, and an
electric lamp is lighted, which signals cannot fail
to attract attention in day-time or at night. By the
opening of the box-lid the tube admits into the
coffin light from the lamp, sufficient air for breathing,
and also serves as a speaking tube."

This highly ingenious contrivance does infinite
credit to the inventor's turn for mechanics. From a
scientific point of view, however, his proposals are
open to serious objection. For instance, if the simple
act of breathing suffices to sound the alarm, and if
every person not dead must breathe, then there would
surely be no need to wait until burial in order to
apply the apparatus, which could be equally well used
as a test at any time after the supposed death. But
perhaps the Chamberlain of the Russian Emperor
believes, as many other advocates of the frequency of
premature burial appear to do, that life may be
maintained for days together without breathing.
Another fatal objection to the apparatus is that
changes of shape occur in all or nearly all dead bodies
as the result of putrefaction. It may be pretty safely
predicted that a delicately adjusted apparatus fitted
on the lines above described would be set going in
nine cases out of ten. At any rate, Count Karnice-
Karnicki may be warned that the mere fact of his
bell and flag being set in action when attached to a
grave would not be accepted as evidence of live burial
by scientifically-minded persons.

Preventive Societies.

These are the days of societies, learned and other-

wise. which spring up on all hands like a plentiful
crop of mushrooms. Of the whole series, however,
there seems to be none whose existence could be less
justifiable than that for the Prevention of Premature
Burial. This association has been organised to com-
bat an evil that has not been shown to exist, a trifling
preliminary that would be considered necessary in
most protective combinations. That it is otherwise
founded on business principles may be gathered from
the fact that it issues a form of bequest, stating that
such and such a legacy is to be paid to the Society.
But if the executors fail to notify the death to the
Secretary, and to carry out his instructions, the whole
of the estate of deceased is to go to the Society.
There are four examining physicians for death verifi-
cation, who are also Vice-Presidents of the Association. The Secretary, a non-medical man, publishes a
book on the "Ars Vivendi" system of curing diseases
and of acquiring mental and bodily vigour. One
wonders whether any subtle connecting link can
possibly exist between the "art of living" and premature burial.

General Conclusions.

We may, then, reviewing the whole situation, safely
conclude :—

1. That in no single case has it been shown that
the signs of death, if properly tested, are fallacious
as a whole.

2. That persons are not often buried alive in this
or any other country.

3. That no case of live burial has been proved
when ordinary skilled precautions have been taken to
prevent such an occurrence.

4. That the mass of reported cases of premature burials in books and journals is worthless from the point of view of exact evidence.

At the same time, it must be admitted that : —

5. There is a remote possibility, hardly amounting to a probability, that in some instances a body might be prematurely buried; especially where hasty burial was necessary, as in hot countries, upon battle-fields, and in time of plague.

Lastly the main general conclusion is that :—

6. The theory of frequent premature burial is un-supported by exact evidence, in other words, it occupies the position of a mere popular belief or fable.

PREMATURE BURIAL.

To the Editor of THE MEDICAL PRESS AND CIRCULAR.

SIR,—In an article on the above subject by Dr. David Walsh, the writer makes the astounding statement that "the whole theory of premature burial is unsupported by a single scientifically-proved instance." What is exactly meant by "scientifically proved" is rather hard to define; but here is one case which is so notoriously well known that it can be very soon ascertained whether it is "scientifically proved" or not. The Countess of Mount Edgecombe was buried in the family vault, and some hours after the interment one of the servants went to the vault to steal the rings which had been left on her hands. By putting the "corpse's" fingers in his mouth in order to remove the rings, he roused the Countess to life. She lived for many years afterwards. This incident was vouched for in a letter I received last Christmas from Sir J. Tollemache Sinclair, Bart. (formerly M.P. for Caithness), who heard it from a grandson of the Countess. Now let Dr. David Walsh prove if he can that this is not "scientifically proved."

The object of the London Association for the Prevention of Premature Burial is not to raise a popular scare on a gruesome topic, but to obtain an improved system of death certification, which at present is admitted by everybody to be in great need of reform.

I am, Sir, yours, &c.,

ARTHUR LOVELL,

Author of " Ars Vivendi," &c., and Sec. L.A.P.P.B.

[The above letter is a type of the loose evidence accepted by the advocates of the theory of premature burial. Any man who advanced in proof of a scientific proposition hearsay evidence of what happened three generations back would at once become a general laughing-stock. But Mr. Lovell, the writer of the letter, appears to be prepared to go back as far as Pythagoras of Crotona, "about 550 B.C.," for his so-called scientific facts. At any rate, that is the impression we gather from a slip advertisement of his book, " Ars Vivendi," which has been brought to our notice, and which offers treatment by " Psycho-therapeutic " and other unusual methods. Mr. Lovell's name is not to be found in the *Medical Register.* We opine that most ordinary nineteenth century folk will prefer, both in their medical treatment and in the burial of their dead, to be guided by the dictates of exact latter-day science. The legend, whether hailing from the Pythagorean schools or from the drawing-room of a deceased noble grand-dame, no longer finds recognition by the modern scientific worker and thinker.—ED. M. P. & C.]

INDEX.

*9 7 8 3 7 4 1 1 9 7 3 2 1 *